Drugs & Alcohol

D1359838

Bully on Campus & Online

Drugs & Alcohol

Gunman on Campus

Natural Disasters

Navigating Cyberspace

Peer Pressure & Relationships

Protecting Your Body: Germs, Superbugs, Poison, & Deadly Diseases

Road Safety

Sports

Stranger Danger

Terrorism & Perceived Terrorism Threats

Drugs & Alcohol

Kim Etingoff

Mason Crest

Mason Crest
450 Parkway Drive, Suite D
Broomall, PA 19008
www.masoncrest.com

Printed and bound in the United States of America.

First printing
9 8 7 6 5 4 3 2 1

Series ISBN: 978-1-4222-3044-2
ISBN: 978-1-4222-3046-6
ebook ISBN: 978-1-4222-8830-6

Library of Congress Cataloging-in-Publication Data

Etingoff, Kim.
  Drugs & alcohol / Kim Etingoff.
      pages cm. — (Safety first)
  Includes index.
  Audience: Age 10+
  Audience: Grade 4 to 6.
  ISBN 978-1-4222-3046-6 (hardback) — ISBN 978-1-4222-3044-2 (series) 1. Children—Drug use—Juvenile literature. 2. Children—Alcohol use—Juvenile literature. 3. Children—Drug use—Prevention—Juvenile literature. 4. Children—Alcohol use—Prevention—Juvenile literature. I. Title.
  HV5824.C45E84 2014
  613.8—dc23
                                2014003846

Contents

Introduction

No task is more important than creating safe schools for all children. It should not require an act of courage for parents to send their children to school nor for children to come to school. As adults, we must do everything reasonable to provide a school climate that is safe, secure, and welcoming—an environment where learning can flourish. The educational effectiveness and the strength of any nation is dependent upon a strong and effective educational system that empowers and prepares young people for meaningful and purposeful lives that will promote economic competitiveness, national defense, and quality of life.

Clearly adults are charged with the vital responsibility of creating a positive educational climate. However, the success of young people is also affected by their own participation. The purpose of this series of books is to articulate what young adults can do to ensure their own safety, while at the same time educating them as to the steps that educators, parents, and communities are taking to create and maintain safe schools. Each book in the series gives young people tools that will empower them as participants in this process. The result is a model where students have the information they need to work alongside parents, educators, and community leaders to tackle the safety challenges that face young people every day.

Perhaps one of the most enduring and yet underrated challenges facing young adults is bullying. Ask parents if they can remember the schoolyard bully from when they were in school, and the answers are quite revealing. Unfortunately, the situation is no better today—and new venues for bullying exist in the twenty-first-century world that never existed before. A single bully can intimidate not only a single student but an entire classroom, an entire school, and even an entire community. The problem is underscored by research from the National School Safety Center and the United States Secret Service that indicates that bullying was involved in 80 percent of school shootings over the past two decades. The title in this series that addresses this problem is a valuable and essential tool for promoting safety and stopping bullying.

Another problem that has been highlighted by the media is the threat of violence on our school campuses. In reality, research tells us that schools are the safest place for young people to be. After an incident like Columbine or Sandy Hook, however, it is difficult for the public, including students, to understand that a youngster is a hundred times more likely to be assaulted or killed

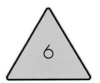

at home or in the community than at school. Students cannot help but absorb the fears that are so prevalent in our society. Therefore, a frank, realistic, discussion of this topic, one that avoids hysteria and exaggeration, is essential for our young people. This series offers a title on this topic that does exactly that. It addresses questions such as: How do you deal with a gunman on the campus? Should you run, hide, or confront? We do not want to scare our children; instead, we want to empower them and reassure them as we prepare them for such a crisis. The book also covers the changing laws and school policies that are being put in place to ensure that students are even safer from the threat of violence in the school.

"Stranger danger" is another safety threat that receives a great deal of attention in the modern world. Again, the goal should be to empower rather than terrify our children. The book in this series focusing on this topic provides young readers with the essential information that will help them be "safety smart," not only at school but also between home and school, at play, and even when they are home alone.

Alcohol and drug abuse is another danger that looms over our young people. As many as 10 percent of American high school students are alcoholics. Meanwhile, when one student was asked, "Is there a drug problem in your school?" her reply was, "No, I can get all the drugs I want." A book in this series focuses on this topic, giving young readers the information they need to truly comprehend that drugs and alcohol are major threats to their safety and well-being.

From peer pressure to natural disasters, from road dangers to sports safety, the Safety First series covers a wide range of other modern concerns. Keeping children and our schools safe is not an isolated challenge. It will require all of us working together to create a climate where young people can have safe access to the educational opportunities that will promote the success of all children as they transition into becoming responsible citizens. This series is an essential tool for classrooms, libraries, guidance counselors, and community centers as they face this challenge.

Dr. Ronald Stephens
Executive Director
National School Safety Center
www.schoolsafety.us

Words to Know

consequences: What happens after you make a choice.
self-destruction: Choices that hurt you rather than help you.

Chapter One

Real-Life Stories

Drugs and alcohol tempt many young people. Kids and teens want to rebel, escape from their lives, or just try something new. But drugs and alcohol, popular tools of rebellion and escape, can have dangerous *consequences*.

One young person knows that firsthand. He tells his story on Reachout.org, a website that gives kids and teens information about issues that are important to them. The website also has lots of personal stories.

The storyteller first started getting into trouble in school. "I was becoming an increasingly bad student and got into smoking pot and skipping school more and more. When I was there, I would be disruptive or mess up in some way."

School didn't really matter to him. Instead, drugs started to matter more and more. All he cared about was hanging out with his friends. The people in his group of friends hated school. They were always ready to have a good time, though—and having a good time usually meant doing drugs.

Looking back, the young man realizes that he was confused and depressed during this time in his life. He didn't know who he really was, and he didn't have any goals. He didn't have any reason for being alive, and so he did drugs to fill in the holes in his life and mind.

9

According to the CDC, about a third of all deaths caused by traffic accidents had alcohol involved in some way. Make sure you're making responsible choices!

Drugs & Alcohol

And then he had a scary experience. His girlfriend's group of friends invited him to get drunk with them on the beach. The plan was for everyone to get so drunk that they passed out on the sand. They'd spend the night on the beach, and then head home in the morning. The young man knew his mother would never approve of the plan, of course, so he lied to her about where he was going and what he would be doing.

On the night of their beach party, his girlfriend picked him up in her car and drove him to a liquor store, where he stole all the alcohol they would need. Then they drove to the secluded beach and started drinking.

As the night wore on, the young man realized he wasn't actually having such a good time. He decided to walk back to his girlfriend's car and go to sleep. His girlfriend gave him her keys, and he staggered away.

Unfortunately, he was too drunk to function very well. He was definitely too drunk to make good decisions. He got in the car and decided to start the engine. He revved the engine for a while, and then he got the idea that he should put it in reverse and turn it around. *I'm driving really well,* he thought to himself, *especially considering I drank a whole bottle of Bacardi rum.* He decided he must not be that drunk after all. It seemed to him that going for a drive would be something really nice to do.

So he pressed his foot to the gas. The car raced down the dead-end street at 70 miles per hour. As he reached the end of the street, he realized he had better put his foot on the brake. Instead, he stomped on the accelerator. The car smashed head on into a house.

The car was wrecked. Flashing lights showed up pretty soon, and the police took the young man to the police station. He spent the night there. When he sobered up, he was just glad he hadn't hurt himself or anyone else.

But he still had to deal with the consequences of what he had done. His girlfriend broke up with him. His parents were angry. He had to go to court.

But the young man had parents who loved him and a best friend who cared about him. They all stood by him, even though they were disappointed in him. He was very thankful for their support.

The court decided the young man needed to attend a seven-week class. Each week, the class had assignments to complete. During the classes, emergency services workers did presentations. One of them was a video of actual crashes. The images were horrifying. The young man couldn't shake them out of his mind. They made him nervous to even get in a car.

But in the end, the experience changed his life for the good. "I was heading down a path of drugs, **self-destruction**, and possibly death," he wrote. "I woke up to the world and who I really was." He had a new sense of his own worth. He was grateful to be alive.

There was a lot of work he had to do, though. He had to rebuild his life and get it back on track. One of the biggest things he needed to do was regain his parents' trust. But he was ready to get to work. "That had to be the biggest learning experience of my life," he wrote, "and has defined me forever. I am so happy for who I am now and where I am going. . . . I wouldn't have chosen this experience if I had the choice, but this is what it took to shake me into reality."

According to the FBI, in 2011 there were 1.2 million arrests for driving under the influence. Many offenders drive drunk multiple times before they're caught.

Drugs & Alcohol

Drinking and Driving

Getting drunk can be dangerous. And getting drunk and driving is extra dangerous. About two thousand young people die every year in the United States from car accidents while driving. Among people of all ages, alcohol is involved in about one-third of all car accident deaths. If people didn't drink and drive, we could avoid up to ten thousand deaths every year!

The young man recommends that others not take the same route he did. He hopes that instead people will learn from his story not to make the same mistakes he did.

This story is a lot like other young people's. This young man was actually lucky, because some stories have far more tragic endings.

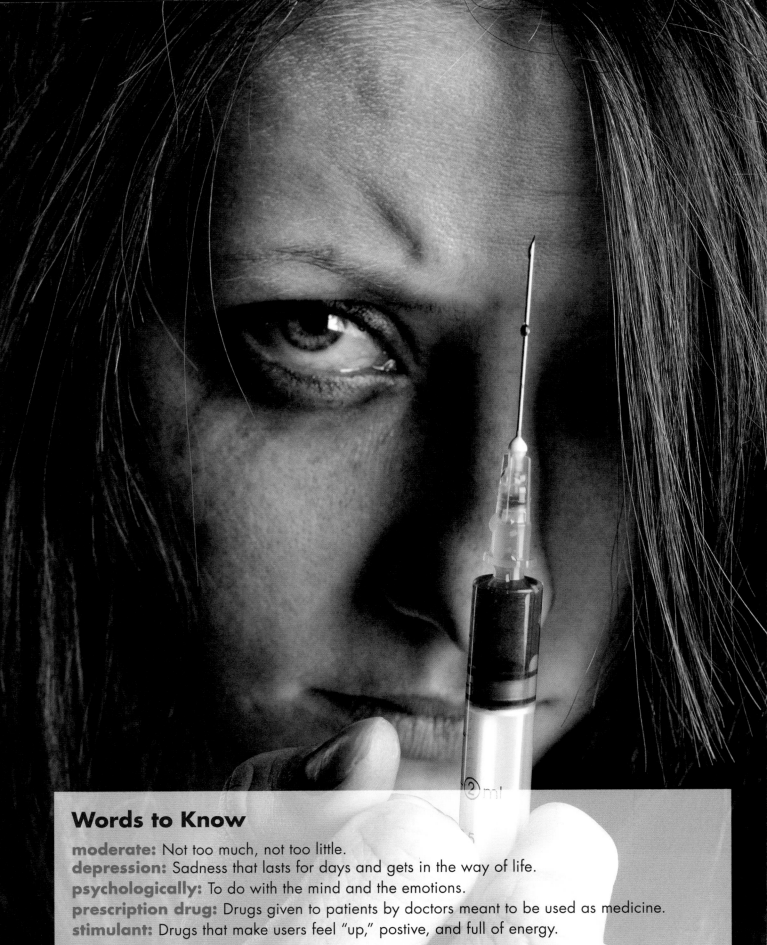

Words to Know

moderate: Not too much, not too little.
depression: Sadness that lasts for days and gets in the way of life.
psychologically: To do with the mind and the emotions.
prescription drug: Drugs given to patients by doctors meant to be used as medicine.
stimulant: Drugs that make users feel "up," postive, and full of energy.

Chapter Two

What Makes Drugs and Alcohol Dangerous?

Adults tell kids all the time, "Drugs and alcohol are dangerous. Don't do them." Are they just being annoying? Do they just not want you to have fun while you're young?

Nope. They're telling the truth. But don't take an adult's word for it. Learn about drugs and alcohol yourself. The more you know, the more you'll start to see how they can mess you up.

USE AND ABUSE

Some people use drugs. And some abuse them. You might find it hard to tell the difference.

Drugs are substances people take that have specific effects on the body. Many drugs are medicines and used to treat sickness. Take cough syrup, for example. You might take a little cough syrup a few times to treat a cough. When you do, you are using a drug. As long as you follow the directions on the label, you are being healthy and safe.

However, some young people abuse cough syrup. They take too much of it at once to get high. They aren't using it as medicine. Getting high on cough syrup is drug abuse.

Addiction is extremely hard to escape from. Luckily, there are communities of people and facilities who know what it's like to go through addiction and how best to help someone who is experiencing it.

Drugs & Alcohol

Drugs and the Brain

Most drugs change how the brain works. Nerve cells in your brain—called neurons—communicate with each other by sending signals. Neurons "talk" by sending and receiving chemicals called neurotransmitters between them. Some drugs help fix problems with how neurons communicate. Other drugs get in the way of normal neuron communication and cause problems. Marijuana, for example, has chemicals that act a lot like neurotransmitters already in your brain. They trick neurons into thinking they are brain neurotransmitters. Amphetamines works differently. They make neurons release many neurotransmitters all at once. Both drugs involve neurotransmitters that make you feel good. Your brain wants to feel good, so you end up taking more and more drugs.

For some drugs, anytime you take them is abuse. Heroin doesn't treat any sicknesses, so we don't use it as medicine. Since there are no medical benefits with heroin, anytime you use it is abuse. And heroin is very dangerous. In fact, it is so dangerous that selling, buying, and using it are against the law.

The line between use and abuse is harder with other drugs. What about coffee? The caffeine in coffee is a drug; many people drink coffee to feel more awake and energetic. Drinking one cup of coffee in the morning seems like a **moderate** and safe use of caffeine. One cup of coffee might become two in the morning. And another in the afternoon. Pretty soon, you need coffee all the time. Your use of coffee became abuse. It's up to you and the people who care about you to decide when you've crossed the line.

ADDICTION

Addiction is a step beyond abuse. Many drugs make you want more of them. When you feel like you can't live your life without more drugs, you've become addicted.

Drug abuse can lead to a couple kinds of addiction. One is physical addiction. The first time a person takes a certain drug, she might feel really, really good. The drug is working with her brain to make her feel good.

If she keeps using the drug, her brain and body gets used to it. She needs more and more of the drug to feel as good as she did the first time.

And if she stops taking the drug, she feels really bad. She goes through withdrawal—shaking, headaches, nervousness, **depression**, a racing heart, and more. The withdrawal symptoms depend on the drug and the person. A person who abuses a drug—or more than one drug—keeps using, so she doesn't end up feeling all these things.

Someone who abuses drugs may also become **psychologically** addicted to them. If he needs a drug to feel good, he is psychologically addicted. He might need a drug to have a good time with friends. Or to not feel sad. Or to escape from problems at home.

Students who use drugs or alcohol are more likely to do poorly in school. Many drugs affect your mind in ways that make it hard to concentrate, or they fill up time you should be spending on schoolwork.

Drugs & Alcohol

A person who becomes addicted to drugs might have one or both types of addiction. They usually aren't easy to separate. Both kinds make life very hard.

People who are addicted to a drug crave it a lot of the time. Sometimes all the time. They spend a lot of time thinking about the drug, getting it, and using it. They spend a lot of money buying it. They aren't free to lead their own lives when addicted to drugs.

Starting to use drugs and alcohol at a young age could lead to addiction. One scientific study focused on kids and young teens who drank alcohol. The study found that people who started drinking before fifteen were much more likely to become addicted to alcohol. People who waited until they were twenty-one to drink alcohol were much less likely to become addicted.

Almost every drug can lead to addiction. Nicotine, alcohol, and caffeine are very addictive, legal drugs. Heroin and cocaine are addictive but illegal. Other drugs can be addictive, too. Many people argue that marijuana isn't addictive. However, some scientists say marijuana users can become psychologically addicted over time.

UNPLEASANT SIDE EFFECTS

Drugs are supposed to make you feel good. That's why people take them. They want the "high" drugs give them.

But don't be fooled. Drugs don't always make you feel good. Sometimes they make you feel really bad. And you'll never know how you'll respond to a drug before you take it.

You might not like what a drug does to you. Alcohol might make your heart race. If you drink too much, you might feel sick to your stomach and throw up. If you smoke marijuana, you might cough a lot or burn your mouth or throat. You might feel like you're losing control of your life while you're tripping on a hallucinogenic drug. Taking drugs can be scary and unpleasant.

DOING POORLY IN SCHOOL

One big consequence of drugs and alcohol is doing worse in school. Even in the best of times, school can be hard. You have to do your homework and study. You have to pay attention in class.

Drugs make that a lot harder. Instead of paying attention in class, a person who abuses drugs may be thinking about getting high. Or the drug he's doing might make paying attention physically more difficult. Marijuana, for instance, can cloud your brain and make remembering and paying attention harder.

Doing drugs and drinking take up time. After school and on weekends, you should be spending some time doing homework or studying. Drug abusers use that time to trip or get drunk.

You don't have to worry only about the time you lose while you're under the influence of a drug. You also have to worry about what happens after the drug wears off.

People who get drunk often get a hangover the next day. People with hangovers can have headaches. Their stomachs might hurt. They're tired and grumpy. That doesn't sound like a good way to start a school day.

After a while, young people who use drugs notice their grades start to slip. They haven't been doing their homework. They haven't been studying for tests. Maybe they're sneaking out during breaks to take drugs or take a drink from a container hidden in their lockers. They aren't learning, so they aren't getting good grades.

AVOIDING PROBLEMS

Drugs and alcohol help you avoid your problems. On the surface, that seems like a good thing! Who wouldn't want to be happy all the time and avoid difficult things like poor grades, fights with friends, or problems at home?

Think of it this way. Say you're having a fight with a friend. Your friend is mad because you told another friend he was a bad soccer player. He ended up hearing about what you said. Now he's upset and is spreading rumors about you.

You have a couple ways of dealing with your problem. You could start drinking or doing drugs. Maybe you smoke some pot so you'll calm down. Or drink a lot so you get drunk and forget what happened.

But the next day, the problem is still there. Your friend is still mad and spreading rumors. And you're still mad at him.

Or you could learn how to deal with your problem. You could apologize to your friend. And you could learn that saying mean things about someone behind his back isn't a good idea. Your friend stops being mad and stops spreading the rumors. You solved your problem.

Many young people do drugs or drink to avoid problems more serious than this one. They are abused at home. Or they're depressed. Or a relative or friend just died. But drugs and alcohol just make those problems worse. They don't teach someone how to deal with the problems.

We all have problems in life. We can't avoid them. You might as well learn how to deal with them while you're young. Drugs don't help you do that at all. Thy only complicate things.

Crystal shared her story on ReachOut.org. She had a serious problem—her brother died in a motorcycle accident.

She says, "Well, my mom went into her own grief and turned a blind eye to me. I did whatever I wanted and stayed out as late as I wanted. Crystal handled her own grief by using drugs. She missed her brother—so she got high. She was angry with her mother for ignoring her—so she used drugs some more. She started out using marijuana, but after a while the high she got from it wasn't enough for her—so she switched to alcohol. When getting drunk no longer gave her the sense of escape she craved, she started using pills.

Her mother found out Crystal was using pills and was angry, but by this time, Crystal was too mixed up to think straight. All she knew was that she was sad and angry. Something inside her pushed her to go even farther. So she did. She started smoking crack.

Eventually, luckily, she got help. And now she gives advice to other young people. "Drugs don't numb pain. They push it to the side until you're sober, and the feelings are too raw and too hard to deal with without the drugs. You can't even have 'fun' without drugs, and you make yourself so sick that you believe you can't do anything without them." Crystal learned her lesson.

Drug use can have a negative impact on your relationships. Problems can get worse and worse until you can't fix them anymore, leaving you all alone.

What Makes Drugs and Alcohol Dangerous?

21

Each year, millions of people are arrested for drug- and alcohol-related reasons. Many of these people will go to prison.

CRIME

Young people who take drugs might not be thinking about jail. Smoking a joint, drinking a beer, or taking a *prescription drug* to get high just seems like something fun and daring to do. But drug use can get you in some serious trouble.

Abusing most drugs is illegal. If you get caught abusing a drug, you could get arrested. You might get a record, which might make it more difficult to get into college or get a job later. You might get expelled from school. You might even be sent to jail.

Lots of things can get you in trouble with the law. Using drugs definitely will. So will selling drugs to other people. Or making or growing your own drugs.

Some people steal money to pay for drugs. Buying drugs or alcohol to support a habit gets expensive! People pay hundreds or even thousands of dollars a month to abuse drugs. Some of them get desperate. They steal money from other people. Or they mug someone. Some may even threaten others with a gun or knife to get money. All these things will get you in huge trouble.

Drugs and alcohol can make you do many things you wouldn't normally do, including acting violent and getting into fights.

Drugs and alcohol make people act in ways they otherwise wouldn't act. People under the influence of drugs might act silly or confused. Sometimes they act violent. Violence is never the answer to a problem. And it can definitely get you in trouble with the law.

Drugs and alcohol can make you angry. They can make you get into a fight. Add knives or guns, and drugs are even more dangerous.

People can become violent when they are addicted to a drug. They are willing to do anything to get the drug and get high. They're even willing to hurt or kill others. Without drugs, we'd have a lot less violence and crime in the world.

LONG-TERM HEALTH PROBLEMS

You've probably heard how much drugs and alcohol can hurt your health. It's true! Taking them for a long time can really mess you up. Sometimes taking a drug just one time can be dangerous to your health.

What Makes Drugs and Alcohol Dangerous?

Marijuana might seem harmless compared to other drugs, but it can still have many negative effects on your health and life.

Every drug does something to you. Drinking too much alcohol over a period of time can damage your liver. Doctors think too much alcohol might also play a part in heart disease and some cancers. Sniffing glue can cause hearing loss and kidney damage. Tobacco can cause lung, mouth, and throat cancers. The list goes on and on.

And drugs can lead to death. Heroin and ecstasy can kill you. You can die if you drink too much alcohol at once. Just trying one of these drugs once can kill you.

Many people with drug addictions get depressed. Depression is extreme sadness. Those who are depressed aren't able to live normal lives. Some of them end up deciding to end it all. Sadly, there have been many drug abusers and addicts who have killed themselves because of depression and other bad feelings.

Drugs & Alcohol

SPOTLIGHT ON ALCOHOL

More people use alcohol than any other kind of drug. Alcohol is so common that we often don't even think of it as a drug. And for people age twenty-one and over, alcohol is legal.

People can use alcohol wisely. A drink at dinner or out with friends can be part of a healthy life. Moderate alcohol use isn't usually a problem for adults.

Alcohol can also be part of very unhealthy decisions. Many young people feel a lot of pressure to drink to be cool, to have fun, or to forget their problems. They break the law by drinking and may get in trouble with police.

Alcohol abuse also leads to more problems. People who are drunk may get more violent or sadder. They may be more willing to take risks, like having unprotected sex or driving too fast. Too much to drink in a short period of time can cause alcohol poisoning, which can kill.

SPOTLIGHT ON MARIJUANA

Lots of people think marijuana isn't dangerous. They think it's a harmless drug. While it's true that marijuana won't hurt you like heroin or cocaine, it can still cause problems in your life.

People use marijuana to feel a high. Marijuana is especially attractive to people with problems they don't want to deal with. Users feel happier and calmer. And marijuana is often easier to get and inexpensive compared to other drugs.

Though it may make people feel better, marijuana has plenty of bad side effects. People who smoke marijuana (or take it in any other form) often have fuzzier memories. They have trouble thinking clearly. Long-term abusers can end up with memory loss.

Marijuana is sometimes used legally for medicinal purposes. For example, doctors in some states can give cancer patients marijuana to help them want to eat more.

As of 2014 in the United States, two states have even made marijuana legal. However, that doesn't mean marijuana is completely safe. Just like alcohol, marijuana can still be dangerous and should be used wisely in those states.

SPOTLIGHT ON PRESCRIPTION DRUGS

Some kids and teens turn to prescription drugs if they want to get high. They think since prescription drugs are legal, it must be OK. People take prescription drugs to treat sickness, so they think they must be safer. They are also often easier to get than other drugs.

Prescription drugs are definitely not safer than other drugs. And prescription drug abuse is illegal. If you are using a drug without a prescription written specifically for you, you are breaking the law.

People abuse all sorts of prescription drugs. Painkillers are common, like Vicodin. So are *stimulant* drugs, like Adderall. Used properly, as prescribed by a doctor for a medical condition, they are safe. If you don't, they can be addictive and dangerous.

Words to Know

rehab: Short for "rehabilitation," rehab is a place where addicts can stop using drugs and learn to live without using them.

counselor: A person who talks with and listens to people struggling with drug abuse in order to help them move past addiction.

Chapter Three

Staying Safe and Being Prepared

Here's a story from the website for the National Council on Alcoholism and Drug Dependence (NCADD). A young woman named Allison describes how she chose to move past drug abuse and inspire others to do the same. For her, *rehab* was a lifesaver.

FINDING HOPE

When she was eighteen, Allison entered rehab. "Alcohol was my drug of choice," she says, "but I smoked pot, popped pills, used acid, crack, cocaine—whatever I could get my hands on. It wasn't about a particular drug. I just wanted to escape, get away from being me, so to speak. I started drinking when I was fourteen."

At first, Allison was skeptical that rehab would do her any good. She was also a little scared about it. She had heard rumors that the people who ran the rehab would force her to do crazy things. But she agreed to stay for thirty days. Allison didn't really have any other choices left to her. Drugs had ruined her life. She knew if she didn't get help, she was going to end up dead.

Before she ended up in rehab, she had been living in a cheap motel in Florida. She could reach the refrigerator from the bed, so she would roll over in the morning and grab a drink before her feet

Group therapy—talking with others who have an addiction problem—is one way to teach people the skills they need to deal with problems in their lives, without turning back to drugs and alcohol.

Drugs & Alcohol

hit the floor. She'd have another drink in the shower. One morning, she realized she had somehow lost every pair of shoes she owned. She was broke, so she couldn't go out and buy another pair.

She left the hotel and started begging. The hot ground burned her feet. She was tired and scared and sick of her life. Finally, she called her mom. Allison wanted to go home—and she knew she needed help.

Asking for help is often the first step toward recovery. Her mother came down from New York, and before Allison barely knew what was happening, she found herself in rehab.

After a while, Allison got used to life in rehab. She realized that the people there were going to hold her accountable for her actions. They treated her with respect, as an adult, but they weren't going to let her get away with anything. They confronted her with the reality of her choices. Allison got in fights with them, but they kept trying. They didn't give up on her, and slowly, Allison began to learn a new way to live. She hated it—but she also loved it.

The people who had been in rehab longer than Allison had a lot to teach her too. They became her role models. She started to understand why she had started using drugs and alcohol in the first place—and she learned better ways to cope with her problems.

For the first time in her life, Allison had real friends, friends who told her the truth and helped her. They gave her the courage to rebuild her relationships with her family. She learned how to get along with her father and mother, her brother and sister.

While she was in rehab, she also had the opportunity to go to college. On the first day of class, she was so nervous, she almost turned around and left the campus. Instead, she opened up the lunch her roommate had packed her. Inside, she was surprised to find many sheets of paper—and on each one was a note. Every resident and staff member at the rehab had wished her luck on her first day of school. Allison started to cry. People truly cared about her, she realized.

Her nervousness disappeared. She felt better than she had in years. With her head high, she walked into the classroom. She was sober, and she was free.

Allison went on to graduate from rehab and finish school. She became a substance abuse *counselor*. She wanted to help other people struggling with drugs. To top it off, she even started working at her old rehab center!

To make sure she stays sober, she goes to therapy. She goes to Alcoholics Anonymous (AA), a group that helps addicts stay off alcohol.

Allison ends her story by saying, "I love my job and I love my life. Most important, I love the rehab facility for helping me become the woman I am today."

Allison's story points out lots of things that can help people fight drug abuse. She ended her drug abuse with rehab and the support of friends and family. Professional help is important. Drug abusers who have become addicted especially need professional help. Doctors can help. Live-in rehabilitation centers also help. So do therapists and social workers.

PREVENTING DRUG ABUSE

The best way to fight drug abuse, including alcohol abuse, is to stop it from happening in the first place! Preventing drug abuse means we'll avoid all the problems drugs cause.

Many schools have banned drugs from their campuses, but it's also important to teach both kids and adults why drugs can be harmful to their lives.

Drugs & Alcohol

Teaching younger kids about the dangers of drugs in schools helps them to make educated decisions when they get older.

Schools and communities all over the world have drug use prevention programs. The programs teach young people about the dangers of drugs. People who run the programs hope that by educating young people about drugs, they'll choose not to do them. But do drug use prevention programs really work?

Many of them do! The National Institute on Drug Abuse published a handbook titled *Preventing Drug Use Among Children and Adolescents*. It gives many examples of programs that work.

For example, researchers have shown that a program called Life Skills Training (LST) can work. Young people in middle school go through the LST program for three years in a row. There's also an LST program for elementary school students. Students learn how to say no to drugs. They learn the dangers of doing drugs.

The LST program teaches more than just saying no to drugs, which is why it works. Students also learn how to feel good about themselves and have good self-esteem. And they learn how to deal with their problems. When young people feel good about themselves and know how to deal with problems, they're less likely to do drugs.

Researchers found the LST program actually prevented young people from doing drugs. Many fewer students ended up abusing drugs than if they hadn't gone through the program.

The handbook outlines some of the things that make drug use prevention programs, like LST, work. Successful programs often work with families and at school. Talking to young people through their families and through school works better than just working with one or the other.

LST programs help people make good decisions to live healthy lives, which builds self-confidence. Self-confident young people experience more success, which in turn makes them less likely to turn to drugs.

Drugs & Alcohol

Successful programs also last a long time. A program might start teaching kids about drugs in elementary school. If no one talks to the same young people in middle school and high school, more end up abusing drugs. A good program will follow young people all the way from childhood to teens.

Successful programs also are interactive. If someone stands at the front of your classroom and talks at you for an hour, you probably won't pay attention. You'll be bored. But if the teacher asks you to perform a skit or draw something, you'll learn a lot better. You'll pay attention and remember what you learned about drugs.

Programs like these are all about you and your future. They teach you ways to stay safe!

Chapter Four

What Can You Do to Stay Safe?

Drugs and alcohol are a real part of growing up. You might not use them, but you may know someone who does. Or you've been pressured to use them. Or you've already tried them.

No matter what your relationship to drugs is, it pays to learn more about them. Then you can make the right choice to stay safe and healthy.

SAYING NO

If you don't use drugs, congratulations! You are choosing to be safe and smart. You know you don't need drugs to be happy or have fun. In fact, you probably know drugs won't make you happy at all.

But just because you don't use them doesn't mean you won't be tempted to some day. You might make a new friend who does drugs or drinks alcohol. Or you might become curious about what taking drugs is like.

Stay strong. Learn everything you can about drugs. And tell yourself you're making the right decision not to do them.

35

People who have had problems with drugs and alcohol in their own lives know how to support those who are having those problems now.

Drugs & Alcohol

It can be hard to say no to drugs if your friends are pressuring you—you might want to be cool or might not want to risk ruining your friendship.

Adults can tell you all sorts of ways to say no to drugs. You can ignore the person asking. Give them a reason you don't want to use. Change the subject.

But the fact is, you have to first make the decision you don't want to use drugs. Before someone ever asks you, you have to know what your answer is going to be.

You have plenty of good reasons not to start using drugs. You want to stay healthy. You want to avoid addiction. You want to do well in school. You want to be the best person you can be. Remind yourself of those reasons whenever you can.

Even if you have already tried drugs, it's never too late to say no. You don't have to keep using them. Start fresh and stay sober. Get help.

ADVICE

Many young people who have gone through drug or alcohol abuse want to help others. They share their stories so other young people can avoid the mistakes they made.

Several young British people share their advice on youthhealthtalk.org. Jen, for example, says

When you say no to your friends, you might end up upsetting the people close to you—but it's still important for you to make decisions that are healthy for yourself!

Drugs & Alcohol

Test Yourself

1. Have you ever felt like you should cut down on your drinking or drug use?
2. Have you ever felt irritated by criticism of your drinking and drug use?
3. Have you ever felt guilty about your drinking, drug use, or behavior during its use?
4. Do you ever take a drink or use drugs in the morning?

If you answered yes to one of these questions, the possibility that you are alcohol or drug dependent is significantly increased. This may also mean that although you are not dependent on drugs or alcohol at this time, you could become dependent if your pattern of abuse continues.

If you answered yes to two of these questions, it is very likely that you are dependent on drugs or alcohol.

If you answered yes to three or four of these questions, there is a greater than 95 percent chance that you are dependent on drugs or alcohol. Please seek assistance for your drug or alcohol problem immediately.

(*Source*: Florida Institute of Technology, *www.fit.edu/caps/articles/facts.php*.)

it is important to not cave into peer pressure. "Just don't feel pressured into anything." Jen knows that when you're young, what your friends think seems like a big deal. The need to fit in makes you do things you're not really comfortable doing. Her advice to teachers and parents: give kids a safe environment where they can talk honestly about their worries. Open communication will help young people know that they have more alternatives than whatever their group of friends are telling them to do.

On the same website, Chloe wrote, "Make sure you are educated and informed correctly. Don't take your friend's word for it." Friends aren't experts on life. They don't understand the consequences of using drugs and alcohol. They're too inexperienced to realize that drugs and alcohol don't make your problems go away. Instead, drugs and getting high will probably make your problems even worse.

Steph used the same website to remind kids to think about the risks of getting high or drunk. When you're in that state, you aren't aware of what's going on around you. You won't be able to keep yourself safe. You can decide to do stupid things that could hurt you or others—and you might end up in a dangerous situation where you can't keep other people from hurting you.

QUITTING

Trying to quit drugs is hard for most people. Let's say you've been smoking cigarettes, which have the addictive drug nicotine in them. You started smoking because your new friend told you it was

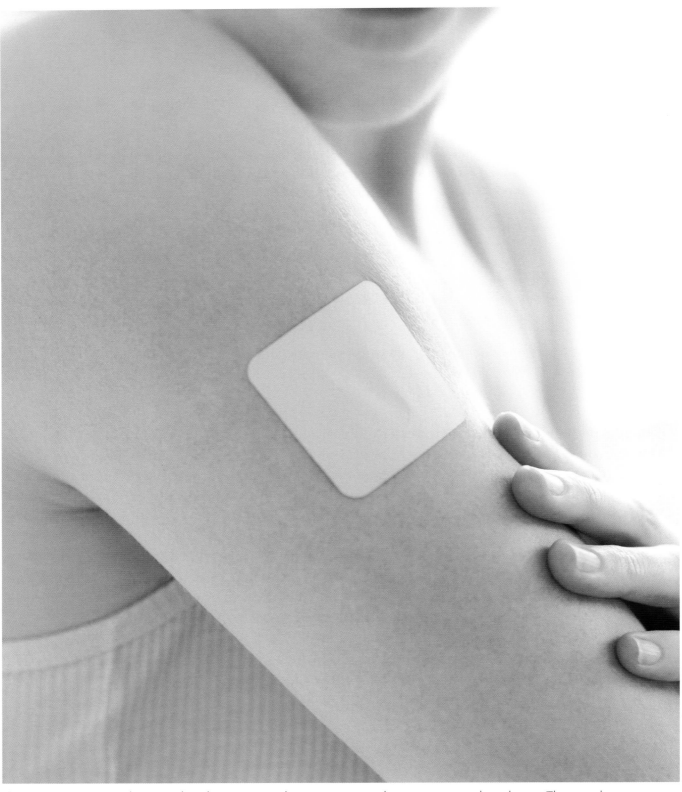

There are many products and techniques out there to quit smoking or using other drugs. The patch is one way to get help giving up smoking.

Drugs & Alcohol

What Not To Do

The National Council on Alcoholism and Drug Dependence (www.ncadd.org) offers a list of things not to do when dealing with friends who abuse drugs.

- Don't Preach: Don't lecture, threaten, bribe, preach, or moralize.
- Don't Be a Martyr: Avoid emotional appeals that may only increase feelings of guilt and the compulsion to drink or use other drugs.
- Don't Cover Up: Don't lie, or make excuses for them and their behavior.
- Don't Assume Their Responsibilities: Taking over their responsibilities protects them from the consequences of their behavior.
- Don't Argue When Using: When they are using alcohol or drugs, they can't have a rational conversation.
- Don't Feel Guilty or Responsible: Their behavior is not your fault.
- Don't Join Them: Don't try to keep up with them by drinking or using.

cool. When you smoke, you can hang out with your new friend and all her friends. You feel like you belong to the group.

But you don't really have enough money to smoke cigarettes all the time. They're expensive! You spend all your allowance on them. You even steal money from your family to buy them. And since it may be illegal for someone your age to buy them, you sometimes steal them, too.

And you don't really like how they make you feel. You've been coughing a lot. And your teeth are getting yellow. You're worried about getting lung cancer or some other disease someday.

So you decide you want to stop smoking. You try stopping all at once, but it doesn't work. You're addicted to the nicotine, so your body craves more. Plus, you still want to hang out with your friends, who are all smoking.

This is a pretty typical story. Quitting cigarettes or other drugs is hard! Most people have to try a few times before they really quit.

You'll find it easier to quit if you hung out with different people. You won't feel pressure to smoke. Tell everyone you know you're trying to quit. Your real friends will help you quit. They won't make fun of you or tell you to keep smoking.

You can also talk to a guidance counselor, doctor, or psychiatrist about quitting. They're all people who can help you and give you good advice.

There are lots of resources out there to help you quit using drugs. Alcoholics Anonymous, Narcotics Anonymous, and Cocaine Anonymous can all help you. Look online to find the closest chapter to where you live.

You can also call drug and alcohol helplines. You'll speak to someone on the phone who will tell you where to get help. Try the National Alcoholism and Substance Abuse Information Center at (800) 784-6776 in the United States or the National Kids Help Phone at (800) 668-6868 in Canada.

When someone is trying to quit using drugs or alcohol, it helps a lot for her to have the support of her friends and family.

Drugs & Alcohol

When you're trying to help your friend stop using drugs, don't get in an argument. Make sure she knows she has your support and that you care about her.

FRIENDS IN TROUBLE

What if you have a friend who is abusing drugs or alcohol? Your friend needs your support. Don't just stop hanging out with her, because she's making some bad decisions. Stick around, and see if you can offer some help.

Tell your friend you're worried about him. Tell him why. Even if he gets mad, know you're doing the right thing. Maybe he doesn't know his drug abuse is a problem. Or maybe he's too scared to stop. He might find it easier to stop using drugs if he knows someone is on his side.

If you don't speak up, the drug abuse will get worse and worse. Your friend will someday realize she's making a mistake. But by then, she could have gone through some pretty tough stuff. Talk to her about her drug abuse now, not later.

When you talk to someone about his drug abuse, be careful. You don't want to make it sound like you're judging him. You do want to sound like you care a lot about him and support him. Don't say, "You're stupid for using drugs." Say, "I'm worried about how many drugs you're using."

Helping friends or family who abuse drugs is hard. They can be ungrateful and mean to you

You are probably going to encounter drugs and alcohol at some point in your life—but if you learn how to make good choices and say no to them, you can stay happy and healthy.

Drugs & Alcohol

if you tell them they need to stop. But they really do need someone who cares about them. Once they get past their drug abuse, they'll thank you. Good friends and family save lives when it comes to drugs.

Drugs and alcohol are a reality. Using or not using is one of the biggest problems you'll face as a young person. Learn to avoid them now, and you'll make healthy choices the rest of your life. Learn the facts. Believe in yourself! Stay away from drugs and lead a happier and healthier life.

Find Out More

ONLINE

Drug Free World
www.drugfreeworld.org/#/interactive

TeensHealth: Drugs and Alcohol
kidshealth.org/teen/drug_alcohol/#cat20138

It's My Life: Drug Abuse
pbskids.org/itsmylife/body/drugabuse

Reachout.com
us.reachout.com

Youthhealthtalk.org
www.youthhealthtalk.org/young_people_drugs_and_alcohol

IN BOOKS

Berry, Joy. *Good Answers to Tough Questions about Substance Abuse.* New York: Joy Berry Enterprises, 2008.

Haughton, Emma. *Drug Abuse? Viewpoint*s. North Mankato, Minn.: Sea to Sea Publications, 2005.

Klosterman, Lorrie. *The Facts about Drugs and the Body.* Pelham, N.Y.: Benchmark Books, 2007.

Powell, Jillian. *Alcohol and Drug Abuse.* New York: Gareth Stevens Publishing, 2008.

Rees, Jonathan. *Drugs.* Vancouver, B.C.: Whitecap Books, 2010.

Index

About the Author & Consultant

Kim Etingoff lives in Boston, Massachusetts. She spends part of her time working on farms, and enjoys writing on topics related to health and nutrition.

Dr. Ronald D. Stephens currently serves as executive director of the National School Safety Center. His past experience includes service as a teacher, assistant superintendent, and school board member. Administrative experience includes serving as a chief school business officer, with responsibilities over school safety and security, and as vice president of Pepperdine University.

Dr. Stephens has conducted more than 1000 school security and safety site assessments throughout the United States. He was described by the *Denver Post* as "the nation's leading school crime prevention expert." Dr. Stephens serves as consultant and frequent speaker for school districts, law enforcement agencies and professional organizations worldwide. He is the author of numerous articles on school safety as well as the author of *School Safety: A Handbook for Violence Prevention*. His career is distinguished by military service. He is married and has three children.

Picture Credits